The Two Octaves Book for Violin

Scales

Arpeggios

Broken Thirds

by Cassia Harvey

Contents

C Major/C Minor.................................. 2
G Major/G Minor.................................. 6
F Major/F Minor....................................10
D Major/D Minor..................................14
B-Flat Major/B-Flat Minor....................18
A Major/A Minor..................................22
E-Flat Major/E-Flat Minor.....................26
E Major/E Minor.................................. 30
A-Flat Major/G-Sharp Minor...............34
B Major/B Minor...................................38
D-Flat Major/C-Sharp Minor............... 42
F-Sharp Major/F-Sharp Minor............46
Chromatic Scales..................................50
Harmonic Minor Scales........................54

CHP265

©2015 by C. Harvey Publications® All Rights Reserved.

www.charveypublications.com - print books & free sheet music blog
www.learnstrings.com - PDF downloadable books & chamber music

Broken Thirds in C Major

C Minor Scale

The Two Octaves Book for Violin

©2015 C. Harvey Publications. All Rights Reserved.

Major/Minor Arpeggios in C

G Major Scale

Broken Thirds in G Major

G Minor Scale

Major/Minor Arpeggios in G

F Major Scale

Broken Thirds in F Major

Major/Minor Arpeggios in F

D Major Scale

Broken Thirds in D Major

D Minor Scale

Major/Minor Arpeggios in D

B♭ Major Scale

Broken Thirds in B♭ Major

B♭ Minor Scale

Major/Minor Arpeggios in B♭

A Major Scale

Broken Thirds in A Major

A Minor Scale

Major/Minor Arpeggios in A

E♭ Major Scale

Broken Thirds in E♭ Major

E♭ Minor Scale

Major/Minor Arpeggios in E♭

E Major Scale

Broken Thirds in E Major

E Minor Scale

Major/Minor Arpeggios in E

A♭ Major Scale

Broken Thirds in A♭ Major

G# Minor Scale

Major/Minor Arpeggios in A♭ and G♯

B Major Scale

Broken Thirds in B Major

B Minor Scale

Major/Minor Arpeggios in B

D♭ Major Scale

Broken Thirds in D♭ Major

C# Minor Scale

The Two Octaves Book for Violin
45

Major/Minor Arpeggios in D♭ and C♯

©2015 C. Harvey Publications. All Rights Reserved.

F# Major Scale

The Two Octaves Book for Violin 47

Broken Thirds in F# Major

©2015 C. Harvey Publications. All Rights Reserved.

48

F# Minor Scale

The Two Octaves Book for Violin

©2015 C. Harvey Publications. All Rights Reserved.

Major/Minor Arpeggios in F#

Chromatic Scales

G chromatic

G♯/A♭ chromatic

A chromatic

The Two Octaves Book for Violin

A♯/B♭ chromatic

B chromatic

C chromatic

©2015 C. Harvey Publications. All Rights Reserved.

The Two Octaves Book for Violin

C♯/D♭ chromatic

D chromatic

D♯/E♭ chromatic

©2015 C. Harvey Publications. All Rights Reserved.

The Two Octaves Book for Violin

E chromatic

F chromatic

F#/Gb chromatic

©2015 C. Harvey Publications. All Rights Reserved.

High G Chromatic

Chromatic Exercise

56

F# minor

C# minor

G# minor

©2015 C. Harvey Publications. All Rights Reserved.

58 — The Two Octaves Book for Violin

C minor

G minor

D minor

©2015 C. Harvey Publications. All Rights Reserved.

Also available from www.charveypublications.com: CHP354
Three-Octave Scales for the Violin, Book One

Part One: Major Scales, Main Fingering

1. G major - Preparatory Shifting

Cassia Harvey

©2019 C. Harvey Publications All Rights Reserved.

www.ingramcontent.com/pod-product-compliance
Lightning Source LLC
Chambersburg PA
CBHW051424070526
44584CB00023B/3566